max science primary

Journal 2

DISCOVERING THROUGH ENQUIRY

PAT DOWER

SERIES EDITOR: **BOB KIBBLE**

macmillan education
INTERNATIONAL CURRICULUM

Macmillan Education
4 Crinan Street
London N1 9XW
A division of Springer Nature Limited

Companies and representatives throughout the world

Journal ISBN 978-1-380-02157-1

First published 2019

Original design by EMC Design Ltd and Macmillan Education
Page make-up by Ink Design
Illustrated by Chris Venter pp 1, 3, 6, 7, 8, 11, 12, 16, 17, 21, 22, 26, 27, 28, 31, 32, 33, 36, 37, 38, 41, 46, 51; Natalie and Tamsin Hinrichsen pp 56, 57, 58, 61, 65, 70, 75, 76, 80
Cover design by Sparks Publishing Services Ltd and Macmillan Education
Cover illustrationby Star Publishing Pte Ltd and Jorge Santillan c/o Beehive Illustration Agency
Picture research by Susannah Jayes

The author and publishers would like to thank the following for permission to reproduce their photographs:
Getty Images/foto-ruhrgebiet p48.

Printed and bound in Brazil
2024
13

Contents

Introducing the *Max Science primary* Journal

The ***Max Science primary* Journal** complements the ***Max Science primary*** series by providing a link between learning at school and learning at home. It matches the topics from the course and the Cambridge Primary Science Curriculum framework with a topic-by-topic series of structured activities for learners to complete with an adult.

As a parent or carer, it is sometimes difficult to know what is being taught in school and how your child is really doing in a subject. Do they enjoy it? Do they understand the concepts and the vocabulary? This Journal lets you spend time with your learner at home in a supportive way and find out how they are doing in science.

Introducing the topic

A cartoon image and question introduces every science topic in a fun and engaging way.

1 Ourselves

1.1 The human body

Some things the same, some things different

Humans are not exactly the same as one another either. We have differences that allow us to tell one another apart.

Look at the cartoon.

Both children have a head.

What other things can you see that are the same?

Check my science

Each topic allows learners to check their understanding through this activity.

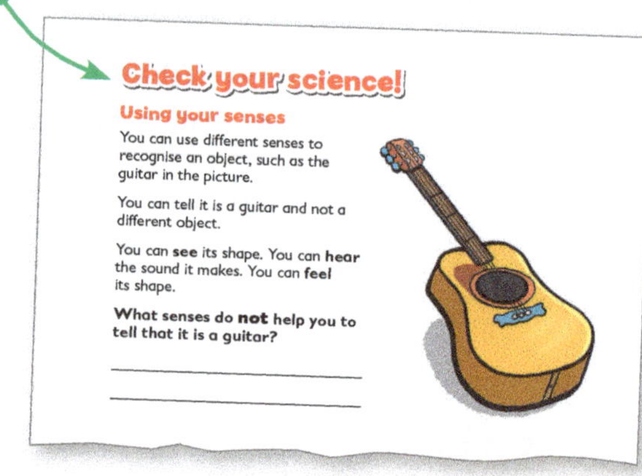
Check your science!

Using your senses

You can use different senses to recognise an object, such as the guitar in the picture.

You can tell it is a guitar and not a different object.

You can **see** its shape. You can **hear** the sound it makes. You can **feel** its shape.

What senses do **not** help you to tell that it is a guitar?

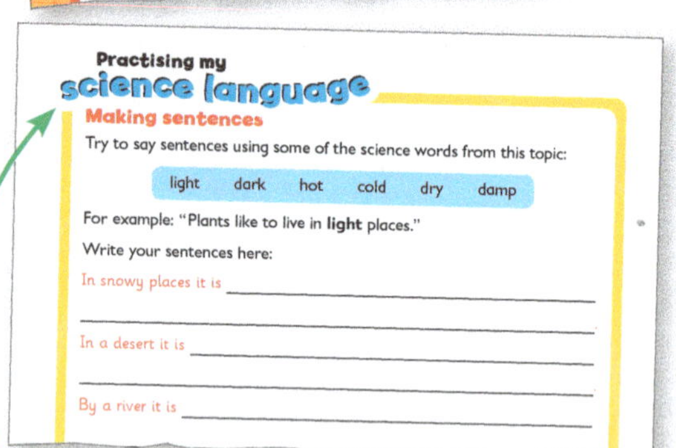
Practising my science language

Making sentences

Try to say sentences using some of the science words from this topic:

light dark hot cold dry damp

For example: "Plants like to live in **light** places."

Write your sentences here:

In snowy places it is

In a desert it is

By a river it is

Practising my science language

This feature provides language practice of key words to improve scientific vocabulary and to make it easier to learn science in English.

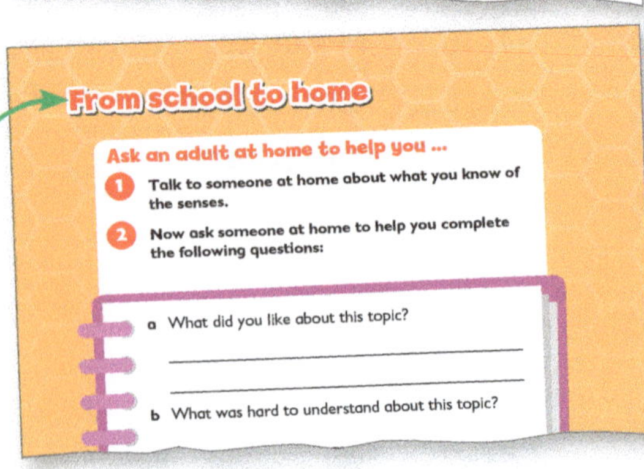
From school to home

Ask an adult at home to help you …

1. Talk to someone at home about what you know of the senses.
2. Now ask someone at home to help you complete the following questions:

a What did you like about this topic?

b What was hard to understand about this topic?

From school to home

You can work together at home to complete this section at the end of each topic. The Journal can then be taken into school for the teacher to look at and discuss, and acts as a record of the learners' progress.

1 Light and dark

1.1 Where light comes from

Some objects give off their own light. The Sun gives off its own light. Other objects only pass on light from elsewhere. They do not give off their own light.

Do you think Omar and Atiya are both right?

Choose one of the options in each sentence.
Then give a reason for your answer.

I think Omar **is right** / **is not right** because ________________________________

____.

I think Atiya **is right** / **is not right** because ________________________________

____.

Check your science!

Look at these three objects.

Table lamp

Shiny spoon

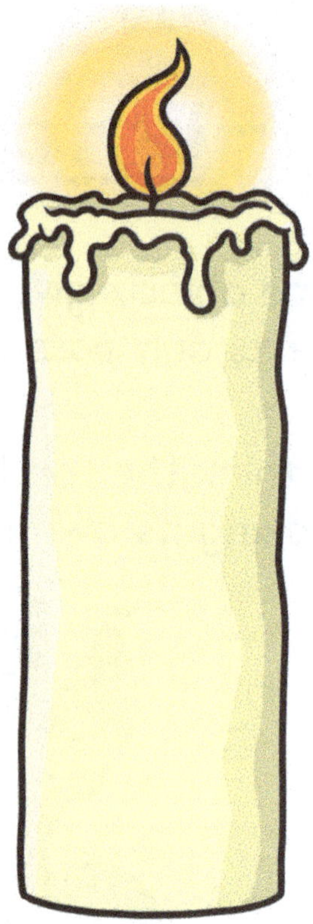

Burning candle

What would these three objects look like if you put them in a room where the Sun was shining through the window?

What would you see if you put the three objects in a dark room?

Practising my

science language

Which bold words will make these sentences correct? Circle your answers.

- You can see a mirror in the **light** / **dark**.
- A torch **takes in** / **gives off** its own light.
- When light shines onto a shiny spoon, the spoon looks **dull** / **bright**.
- When it is completely dark it is **possible** / **impossible** to see.

From school to home

Ask an adult at home to help you ...

1. Talk to someone at home about light and dark and where light comes from.
2. Now ask someone at home to help you complete the following questions:

a What did you like about this topic?

____

____

____

b What was hard to understand about this topic?

____

____

____

I understand.

I understand a bit.

I need more time to understand this.

3 **Look again at the checklist below. How are you doing now? Circle one face for each statement.**

- I can name things that give off their own light.
- I know some objects only pass on light from elsewhere.
- I can describe what "dark" means.
- I can describe the difference between bright light, dim light and darkness.

4 **Ask an adult at home to read and sign this.**

I have checked learning on this topic.

We have shared some understanding at home.

Signed: ______________________

Date: ______________

Teacher comment: ____________________________

____

Date: ______________

1.2 Shadows

When an object blocks light, it causes a shadow. An object can have a shadow only when there is light.

Help Gavin to improve his shadow drawings. Draw your ideas below.

Check your science!

The Sun's position in the sky looks to change during the day. This makes the size and position of shadows change.

Look at this picture. It shows the Sun in three different positions during the day.

Draw the tree's shadow for each position of the Sun. Think about where each shadow should be. Think how long each shadow should be. Label each shadow 1, 2 or 3.

Practising my

science language

Choose the correct words to complete each sentence.

solid shadow different the same longer shorter

dark light behind in front of shines

When an object blocks light it makes a ______________________.

When light shines onto a ______________________ object, a shadow forms ______________________ it.

When the Sun is high in the sky, shadows are ______________________ than when the Sun is low.

Objects of different sizes have shadows that are ______________________.

From school to home

Ask an adult at home to help you ...

1. Talk to someone at home about light and dark and where light comes from.

2. Now ask someone at home to help you complete the following questions:

a What did you like about this topic?

____

____

____

b What was hard to understand about this topic?

____

____

____

I understand. I understand a bit. I need more time to understand this.

3 **Look again at the checklist below. How are you doing now? Circle one face for each statement.**

- I know what a shadow is.
- I can draw shadows correctly.
- I can say what makes shadows.

4 **Ask an adult at home to read and sign this.**

I have checked learning on this topic.

We have shared some understanding at home.

Signed: ______________________

Date: ______________

Teacher comment: ______________________________

____

Date: ______________

2 Electricity

2.1 What does a battery do?

Some objects need a battery to make them work. The battery gives the electricity they need to work.

Yuki is thinking about these three clocks. Which of the clocks work with electricity? Tick the right boxes.

Clock 1 ☐ Clock 2 ☐ Clock 3 ☐

Which of the clocks can work with a battery? Tick the right boxes.

Clock 1 ☐ Clock 2 ☐ Clock 3 ☐

Check your science!

For a bulb to light up, it must be part of a complete circuit.

Look at the pictures showing different parts of a circuit.

Draw how you could put all of these parts together to make the bulb light up.

Why is the bulb holder useful?

Practising my science language

Unscramble these jumbled words:

u i t r c c i _ _ _ _ _ _ _

l u b b _ _ _ _

r s i w e _ _ _ _ _

b e r y a t t _ _ _ _ _ _ _

w o l s f _ _ _ _ _

Choose words from the box to complete these sentences.

circuit electricity light complete wires circle

A battery is a source of ____________________.

I can use ____________ to connect a battery to a light bulb.

This makes a path in which electricity can flow. This path is called a ______________.

If the bulb lights up, I know that the circuit is ______________.

Now read the sentences to someone at home.

From school to home

Ask an adult at home to help you ...

1. Talk to someone at home about what a battery does.

2. Now ask someone at home to help you complete the following questions:

a What did you like about this topic?

____

____

____

b What was hard to understand about this topic?

____

____

____

I understand. | I understand a bit. | I need more time to understand this.

3 **Look again at the checklist below. How are you doing now? Circle one face for each statement.**

- I can name some things that need electricity to work.
- I can say what a battery does.
- I know the parts of a circuit.
- I can build a circuit.
- I can say why a circuit must be complete for a bulb to light up.

4 **Ask an adult at home to read and sign this.**

I have checked learning on this topic.

We have shared some understanding at home.

Signed: ______________________

Date: ______________

Teacher comment: ______________________________

____

Date: ______________

2.2 Exploring circuits

A circuit will only work if all of its parts are arranged in the right way. We say the circuit has to be complete. This means that there should not be any breaks.

Daniel's circuit does not work. What do you think about the ideas from Ed, Asha and Ali? Talk about them with someone at home.

Write some of your own ideas below.

____

____

____

____

Check your science!

Look at the circuits below.

- **Which circuits will work if you add *just one wire*? Draw a tick next to those circuits.**
- **To complete the circuits you ticked, draw in one extra wire on the diagrams.**

Practising my science language

Use some of these words to complete the sentence.

circuit bulb wires battery flows

To make a bulb light up, I have to ______________________________

____

____

____

______________________________.

Try to make more sentences with some of the words.

____

____

____

____

____

____

____

____

From school to home

Ask an adult at home to help you ...

1. Talk to someone at home about circuits.
2. Now ask someone at home to help you complete the following questions:

a What did you like about this topic?

____

____

____

b What was hard to understand about this topic?

____

____

____

I understand. I understand a bit. I need more time to understand this.

3 **Look again at the checklist below. How are you doing now? Circle one face for each statement.**

- I can connect a battery and bulb to make the bulb light up.
- I can predict when a circuit will make a bulb light up.
- I can test my predictions.
- I know that electricity flows in a complete circuit.

4 **Ask an adult at home to read and sign this.**

I have checked learning on this topic.

We have shared some understanding at home.

Signed: ___________________________

Date: ________________

Teacher comment: ___________________________________

____

Date: ________________

2.3 Switches and staying safe

The switch in a circuit can turn something on and off.

Look at the children's questions. Can you help them to understand what a switch does?

Talk about your ideas with someone at home. Write some of your ideas here.

___

___

___

___

Check your science!

Electricity can be dangerous.

Write down what each sign tells you about using electricity safely.

Share these safety rules with someone at home.

Practising my

science language

Switches are found on many objects that use electricity.

Look around your home for objects with switches.

How many objects with switches can you find? ________________

Write the names of some of the objects you found in your own language and in English.

Name of object in your own language	Name of object in English

From school to home

Ask an adult at home to help you ...

1. **Talk to someone at home about switches and staying safe when using electricity.**
2. **Now ask someone at home to help you complete the following questions:**

a What did you like about this topic?

____

____

____

b What was hard to understand about this topic?

____

____

____

I understand. | I understand a bit. | I need more time to understand this.

3 **Look again at the checklist below. How are you doing now? Circle one face for each statement.**

- I can find different kinds of switch.
- I can make a circuit with a switch.
- I know how a switch turns something on or off.
- I know that electricity can be dangerous.
- I know some ways to stay safe when using electricity.

4 **Ask an adult at home to read and sign this.**

I have checked learning on this topic.

We have shared some understanding at home.

Signed: ____________________

Date: ____________

Teacher comment: __________________________

____

Date: ____________

3 Changing materials

3.1 Changing shape

Some materials can change shape. Materials can change shape when we bend, squash, twist or stretch them.

Think about the materials that the objects in the picture are made from.

Can you change the shape of all of these materials easily? Share your ideas with someone at home.

Then write two sentences about your ideas.

____

____

____

____

Check your science!

Tylor is bending this rubber pipe. The action is changing the shape of the material.

What is Tylor doing in these pictures to change the shape of the materials? Use the words from the word box to label the three actions.

twist squash stretch

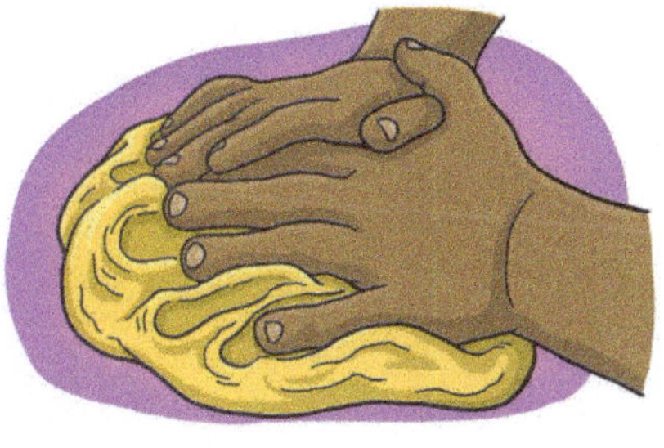

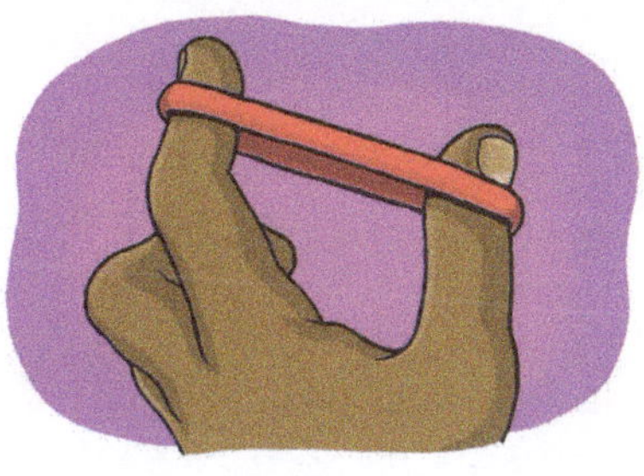

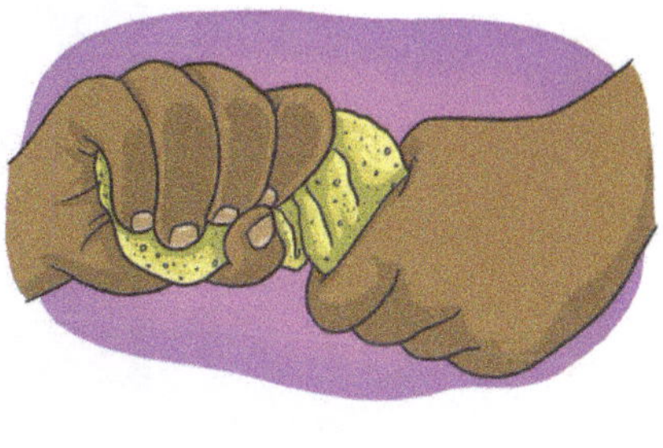

Practising my science language

Think about changing the shape of different materials with your hands.

Read the sentences below. In each sentence, choose one of the bold words from the pairs to make the science correct. The first one has been done for you.

- It is **easy** / **hard** to bend the frame of a carbon fibre tennis racket with your hands.
- It is **easy** / **hard** to squash a piece of modelling clay with your hands.
- It is **easy** / **hard** to twist a rigid iron rod with your hands.
- It is **easy** / **hard** to bend a rope, but it is **easy** / **hard** to stretch it.

From school to home

Ask an adult at home to help you ...

1. Talk to someone at home about changing the shape of materials.
2. Now ask someone at home to help you complete the following questions:

a What did you like about this topic?

____

____

____

b What was hard to understand about this topic?

____

____

____

I understand. I understand a bit. I need more time to understand this.

3. **Look again at the checklist below. How are you doing now? Circle one face for each statement.**

- I can say how a material's shape can change.
- I can predict whether a material's shape will change.
- I can test my predictions.

4. **Ask an adult at home to read and sign this.**

I have checked learning on this topic.

We have shared some understanding at home.

Signed: ______________________

Date: _____________

Teacher comment: ______________________________

____

Date: _____________

3.2 Can heating or cooling change materials?

Some materials change when they get hot or cold.

The children are looking at some materials. What will happen if they heat the materials?

Read what Kassim, Lelina and Aran are saying. Do you agree?

Talk about your ideas with someone at home.

Write your ideas below.

___

___

___

Check your science!

Look at the picture. There are icicles hanging from the building. There is a snowman.

What is happening to the icicles and the snowman?

Why is this happening?

What will happen if the weather turns very cold?

Practising my
science language

Complete these science sentences. Use the words in the box correctly in each one.

An example has been done for you.

baked	boil	droplets	firm	heated	soft	water

- If runny water gets very cold, it turns into ice.
- If ice is ________ it melts. The ice turns into runny ________.
- If dough is ________ in an oven, it becomes ________. It cannot turn back into ________ dough again.
- If water gets very hot, it starts to ________. We can see tiny water ________ rising into the air.

From school to home

Ask an adult at home to help you ...

1. **Talk to someone at home about how materials can change when they get hot or cold.**
2. **Now ask someone at home to help you complete the following questions:**

a What did you like about this topic?

____

____

____

b What was hard to understand about this topic?

____

____

____

I understand.

I understand a bit.

I need more time to understand this.

3 **Look again at the checklist below. How are you doing now? Circle one face for each statement.**

- I know that heating or cooling a material can make it change.
- I can say how water changes when it is heated or cooled.
- I know that some solid materials can melt when they get hot.
- I can investigate how to make a material melt fast or slowly.
- I can record and compare my observations.

4 **Ask an adult at home to read and sign this.**

I have checked learning on this topic.

We have shared some understanding at home.

Signed: ______________________

Date: ______________

Teacher comment: ____________________________

____

Date: ______________

3.3 Dissolving

When some materials are mixed into water, they spread through the water until you cannot see them anymore. This is called dissolving. Not all materials dissolve.

The children want to mix these materials with water to see if they will dissolve.

Read what Vinesh, Riya and Tyra are saying. Who do you think is right?

___

Describe how you can test your answer.

___

___

___

Check your science!

Andrew is testing if a material will dissolve.

The pictures show the steps Andrew followed. But they are in the wrong order.

Stir it.

Look carefully.

Put some of the material into the water.

Get some water.

Write the numbers of the pictures in the correct order to show how to test whether a material will dissolve.

The correct order for the pictures is:

__________ __________ __________ __________

Practising my science language

The sentences below are about dissolving materials.

Read them aloud to someone at home.

When you stir sugar into water, it spreads through the water. You cannot see it anymore. We say the sugar has dissolved.

When you stir sand into water, it does not spread through the water. When you stop stirring, you can still see the sand. It has not dissolved.

Stone and wood are examples of materials that do not dissolve.

Write down any words you find difficult to say or understand.

____

____

Ask someone at home to help you understand the words or practise saying them.

From school to home

Ask an adult at home to help you ...

1. Talk to someone at home about dissolving materials.
2. Now ask someone at home to help you complete the following questions:

a What did you like about this topic?

____

____

____

b What was hard to understand about this topic?

____

____

____

I understand. I understand a bit. I need more time to understand this.

3 **Look again at the checklist below. How are you doing now? Circle one face for each statement.**

- I can say what happens when a material dissolves.
- I can investigate whether a material dissolves or not.
- I can record my results in a table.
- I can name some materials that dissolve.

4 **Ask an adult at home to read and sign this.**

I have checked learning on this topic.

We have shared some understanding at home.

Signed: ______________________

Date: ______________

Teacher comment: ______________________________

____

Date: ______________

3.4 Natural and man-made materials

Natural materials come from the ground or from plants and animals. Wool is a natural material. It comes from an animal.

Some materials are not found naturally on Earth or they are made from other materials. These materials are man-made. Plastic is a man-made material.

Help Hiro and Chun to answer their questions.

Talk about the questions with someone at home.

Write your answers below.

Check your science!

Below is a list of materials. Some are natural materials and some are man-made materials.

Write the materials in the correct column in the table.

glass plastic wood metal wool apple cotton clay

Natural materials	Man-made materials

Practising my

science language

There are six words about materials in the grid below.

Draw a circle around each word that you find.

One has been done for you. **Try to find five more.**

s	n	e	w	o	o	l	l	k	p
d	m	a	n	-	m	a	d	e	j
f	g	c	u	u	g	l	a	s	s
n	a	t	u	r	a	l	u	t	d
s	y	u	i	d	e	r	t	y	i
z	c	m	e	t	a	l	m	l	j
d	u	h	e	s	s	v	g	t	a
d	i	t	c	q	l	e	u	i	f
d	p	l	a	s	t	i	c	l	h

From school to home

Ask an adult at home to help you ...

1. Talk to someone at home about natural materials and man-made materials.
2. Now ask someone at home to help you complete the following questions:

a What did you like about this topic?

____

____

____

b What was hard to understand about this topic?

____

____

____

I understand. I understand a bit. I need more time to understand this.

3 **Look again at the checklist below. How are you doing now? Circle one face for each statement.**

- I can name some natural materials.
- I can say what "man-made" means.
- I can name some man-made materials.

4 **Ask an adult at home to read and sign this.**

I have checked learning on this topic.

We have shared some understanding at home.

Signed: ____________________

Date: ____________

Teacher comment: __________________________

____

Date: ____________

4 Looking at rocks

4.1 Different types of rock

Rocks are natural materials found on and inside the Earth. There are many types, shapes and sizes of rock. Some rocks are very hard. Other rocks are less hard.

Help Amar, Bibek and Tarla sort these materials into two groups.

What feature can you use to sort the materials?

____

Write the letters for the materials in the two shapes below.

Check your science!

Go on a rock hunt where you live. Try to find five different types of rock.

Draw the rocks that you found below. Next to each rock, write where you found it.

Do a test to find out which rock is the hardest and which rock is the softest.

Describe how you tested the hardness of the five rocks.

Label the hardest rock and the softest rock on your drawing.

Practising my science language

The words given below can describe rocks or materials that come from rock.

smooth hard dry round small rough

Choose a word that correctly describes what each material is like. You may use a word only once.

- Rock: ______________________
- Pebbles: ______________________
- Sand: ______________________

Write a sentence using some of the words in the word box. Then read the sentence out loud to someone at home.

____

____

Which word in the box below describes the rock in the picture?

Circle the word.

dull

shiny

soft

From school to home

Ask an adult at home to help you ...

1. Talk to someone at home about different types of rock.
2. Now ask someone at home to help you complete the following questions:

a What did you like about this topic?

____

____

____

b What was hard to understand about this topic?

____

____

____

I understand. | I understand a bit. | I need more time to understand this.

3 **Look again at the checklist below. How are you doing now? Circle one face for each statement.**

- I can compare different types of rock.
- I can compare pebbles, sand and soil.
- I can test how hard a rock is.
- I know of one way that new rocks can form.

4 **Ask an adult at home to read and sign this.**

I have checked learning on this topic.

We have shared some understanding at home.

Signed: ______________________

Date: ______________

Teacher comment: ______________________________

____

Date: ______________

4.2 Natural and man-made building materials

We can use natural materials such as stone for building. People can collect or buy stone close to where they live.

We can also use man-made materials for building. They can be used if there is not enough natural material. Sometimes man-made materials are easier to use.

Read what Ling, Damion and Akmal are saying about the walls.

Write what you think about their ideas here.

___

___

___

Check your science!

Go outside with an adult. Look at the materials used for two different buildings.

List the materials for each building below.

Show whether each material is man-made or natural by drawing a circle around the correct box:

M = man-made

N = natural

Building 1			Building 2		
______	M	N	______	M	N
______	M	N	______	M	N
______	M	N	______	M	N
______	M	N	______	M	N
______	M	N	______	M	N
______	M	N	______	M	N

Draw a picture of one of the buildings you saw. Label the materials.

Practising my science language

Unscramble the letters below to form five words about building materials.

b e p b l e   _ _ _ _ _ _

a m n m a e d -   _ _ _ _ _ _ _ _

l a t r a u n   _ _ _ _ _ _ _

n o s t e   _ _ _ _ _

k c b r i   _ _ _ _ _

Read aloud these four sentences from this topic.

- Bricks are man-made.
- Stone is a natural material.
- Bricks are good for building walls.
- Stone is a hard material.

From school to home

Ask an adult at home to help you ...

1. Talk to someone at home about natural building materials and man-made building materials.
2. Now ask someone at home to help you complete the following questions:

a What did you like about this topic?

____

____

____

b What was hard to understand about this topic?

____

____

____

I understand. I understand a bit. I need more time to understand this.

3 **Look again at the checklist below. How are you doing now? Circle one face for each statement.**

- I can say how to build a strong wall.
- I can name some natural and some man-made building materials.
- I can compare natural and man-made building materials.

4 **Ask an adult at home to read and sign this.**

I have checked learning on this topic.

We have shared some understanding at home.

Signed: ______________________

Date: ______________

Teacher comment: ____________________________

____

Date: ______________

5 Day and night

5.1 Shadows and sundials

You can see shadows on a sunny day. Shadows form when something blocks the light coming from the Sun. Shadows change during the day as the position of the Sun changes.

Read what Jared and Brianna are saying. Think about shadows and the sundial.

- Does it matter where you put a sundial?
- Would the sundial tell the correct time if someone turned it the opposite way round?
- Do sundials always work?

Talk about these questions with someone at home. Write your ideas below.

Check your science!

Look at these pictures of snowmen. Their shadows are missing.

Draw a line from each snowman to its correct shadow.

Practising my

science language

Draw a line to match each word to its correct meaning.

shadow	what something is measured in, for example, metres
night	a darker area where light is blocked
unit	uses the Sun to tell the time
sundial	when the Sun is not shining on your part of the Earth

Look at these pictures. What science ideas do the pictures make you think of?

Write two sentences about science ideas from the pictures.

____

____

____

From school to home

Ask an adult at home to help you ...

1. Talk to someone at home about shadows and how sundials can be used to tell the time.

2. Now ask someone at home to help you complete the following questions:

a What did you like about this topic?

____

____

____

b What was hard to understand about this topic?

____

____

____

I understand. I understand a bit. I need more time to understand this.

3 **Look again at the checklist below. How are you doing now? Circle one face for each statement.**

- I can say how the position and size of a shadow change during the day.
- I understand how the Sun's position causes shadows to change during the day.
- I know how a sundial works.
- I can make my own sundial.

4 **Ask an adult at home to read and sign this.**

I have checked learning on this topic.

We have shared some understanding at home.

Signed: ______________________

Date: ______________

Teacher comment: ____________________________

____

Date: ______________

5.2 Spinning Earth

The Earth spins. This makes it look as if the Sun moves across the sky.

As the Earth spins, our part of the Earth turns away from the Sun. It later becomes nighttime.

As the Earth continues to spin, the Sun comes back into view. This becomes daytime.

Look at the picture. It shows a model of the Sun and the Earth.

- What is playing the part of the Sun in the model?
- Where will it be night on the model of the Earth?
- Where will it be day on the model of the Earth?

Talk about these questions with someone at home.
Write your ideas below.

Check your science!

Tick the sentences that are true.

- The Sun stops shining when we have night. ☐
- It is dark on the side of the Earth facing *towards* the Sun. ☐
- It is dark on the side of the Earth facing *away from* the Sun. ☐
- During the day, the Sun is bright. ☐
- The Sun is always shining, but places do not get light from the Sun all of the time. ☐
- The Earth gives off its own light. ☐
- The Sun gives off its own light. ☐

Practising my science language

Which of the words below describe the movement of the Earth? You can choose more than one. Circle each word you choose.

spin fall drop hit turn stop

Say this rhyme out loud to an adult at home:

It goes dark at night.
That is when there is no light.
The Sun brightly burns
As the Earth turns.

science language

Ask an adult at home to help you ...

1 **Talk to someone at home about the spinning Earth.**

2 **Now ask someone at home to help you complete the following questions:**

a What did you like about this topic?

____

____

____

b What was hard to understand about this topic?

____

____

____

I understand. I understand a bit. I need more time to understand this.

3 **Look again at the checklist below. How are you doing now? Circle one face for each statement.**

- I can say how the Earth moves so that we have day and night.
- I can use clues to help me work out why we have day and night.
- I can use a model to show why we have day and night.

4 **Ask an adult at home to read and sign this.**

I have checked learning on this topic.

We have shared some understanding at home.

Signed: ____________________

Date: ____________

Teacher comment: __________________________

____

Date: ____________

5.3 The Moon

The Moon moves around the Earth. We can see the Moon when it moves above our part of the Earth. We can see the Moon only when there is light from the Sun shining on it.

The children are in different places on the Earth. They all look into the sky at the same time.

Read what they are saying.

Who do you think is right? Why do you think so?
Write your ideas below.

Check your science!

Go outside on four clear nights when you can see stars.

On each night, put a tick in the table below if you can see the Moon. If you can see the Moon, draw what it looks like.

First night	Second night	Third night	Fourth night

Can you always see the Moon at night? Give two reasons to explain your answer.

1. ______________________________

2. ______________________________

The Moon is round but sometimes it can look like it is a different shape.

Why do you think this is?

____

____

____

____

Practising my

science language

Find these six words about day and night in the grid below. They can read forwards, backwards, up or down. Draw a circle around each word that you find. One has been done for you.

Moon Sun turn Earth light

n	o	o	m	m	t	w	p	e	h
a	o	w	o	d	a	h	s	n	w
l	s	g	e	q	a	t	u	r	n
d	f	i	a	p	r	h	n	g	x
h	s	n	r	k	u	n	i	t	i
v	p	n	t	s	h	d	j	y	b
l	i	g	h	t	r	a	j	u	v
s	n	t	y	e	u	r	x	o	w
s	z	a	q	w	o	k	y	m	s

There are two more hidden words.

Can you find them? Circle them in the grid and write them below.

____________________ ____________________

From school to home

Ask an adult at home to help you ...

1. **Talk to someone at home about what you know about the Moon.**
2. **Now ask someone at home to help you complete the following questions:**

a What did you like about this topic?

____

____

____

b What was hard to understand about this topic?

____

____

____

I understand. I understand a bit. I need more time to understand this.

3 **Look again at the checklist below. How are you doing now? Circle one face for each statement.**

- I know that the Moon does not always look the same.
- I understand why the Moon does not always look the same.
- I can describe how the Moon moves.

4 **Ask an adult at home to read and sign this.**

I have checked learning on this topic.

We have shared some understanding at home.

Signed: ______________________

Date: ______________

Teacher comment: ______________________________

____

Date: ______________

6 Plants and animals around us

6.1 Habitats

The places where we find living things are called habitats. A pond is a habitat. A forest is another habitat. Different habitats often contain different living things. This is because the conditions in each habitat are different.

Read what Josue and Oria are saying about the two habitats. Where would you look for living things?

Talk about your ideas with someone at home. Write your ideas below.

____

____

____

____

Check your science!

The tiny animals that you find in habitats are called minibeasts. You can catch minibeasts using a pooter or a pitfall trap.

If you have space outside, make a pitfall trap of your own.

Draw a pitfall trap. Explain how it works.

Practising my

science language

Fill in the gaps in the paragraph using the words below.

suck leaves water fast damp

Some minibeasts live in ponds. They need ______________ to live. A good place to find minibeasts is underneath ____________ and stones. Here it is cool and __________. A pooter is a good way to catch minibeasts that do not move too ____________. You ____________ on the pooter and the minibeast gets caught inside.

Tell someone at home about one or two minibeasts in their habitat.

From school to home

Ask an adult at home to help you ...

1. **Talk to someone at home about what you know about habitats.**

2. **Now ask someone at home to help you complete the following questions:**

a What did you like about this topic?

____

____

____

b What was hard to understand about this topic?

____

____

____

I understand. | I understand a bit. | I need more time to understand this.

3 **Look again at the checklist below. How are you doing now? Circle one face for each statement.**

- I can name three or more different habitats.
- I can describe conditions in different habitats.
- I can say why different animals live in different habitats.
- I know of different ways to catch minibeasts.

4 **Ask an adult at home to read and sign this.**

I have checked learning on this topic.

We have shared some understanding at home.

Signed: ____________________

Date: ____________

Teacher comment: __________________________

____

Date: ____________

6.2 Caring for the environment

Humans can damage the environment. When the environment is damaged, other living things may have nowhere to live.

Read what Hemish, Ame and Darya are saying. What do you think? Is it possible to keep everyone happy?

Talk about your ideas with someone at home. Write your ideas below.

Check your science!

Is the field in the picture a good place to find many different animals?

Tick <u>one</u> of the options below:

- Yes, I think it is a **good place**. ☐
- No, I think it is a **bad place**. ☐
- I am not sure. I think it is **neither a good nor a bad place**. ☐

Talk about the reasons for your answer with someone at home. Write your ideas below.

Practising my science language

Use the clues to solve this crossword.

The words read from left to right, or downwards.
One has been one for you.

Across

1. In a desert, it is ...
3. A name for a small animal
4. A place where humans grow food
5. Rubbish dropped by humans

Down

1. A place where you find living things
2. A lion, a bird and a fish are all ...

From school to home

Ask an adult at home to help you ...

1 **Talk to someone at home about caring for the environment.**

2 **Now ask someone at home to help you complete the following questions:**

a What did you like about this topic?

____

____

____

b What was hard to understand about this topic?

____

____

____

I understand. I understand a bit. I need more time to understand this.

3 **Look again at the checklist below. How are you doing now? Circle one face for each statement.**

- I can describe how humans can damage the environment.
- I can describe how humans can help to protect the environment.

4 **Ask an adult at home to read and sign this.**

I have checked learning on this topic.

We have shared some understanding at home.

Signed: ______________________

Date: ______________

Teacher comment: ______________________________

____

Date: ______________

6.3 Weather

The weather is what it is like outside. Sometimes we have sunny weather. Sometimes we have rainy weather.

Look at what Shera and Rafi have chosen to wear for rainy weather.

Whose choice do you think is best? ______________________________

Which of the items would you choose for sunny, warm weather? Write your ideas below.

____

____

____

____

Check your science!

Draw weather symbols to show these four kinds of weather.

Hot	Snowy
Cloudy	Thunderstorm

Practising my science language

Unscramble the letters below to form five words about weather.

d o l c   _ _ _ _

c i y   _ _ _

d o u l c y   _ _ _ _ _ _

n u s n y   _ _ _ _ _

t o h   _ _ _

Use some weather words to complete these sentences:

- Where I live, the weather is often ____________________ and ____________________.
- At the North Pole, the weather is often ____________________ and ____________________.

From school to home

Ask an adult at home to help you ...

1. **Talk to someone at home about different kinds of weather.**
2. **Now ask someone at home to help you complete the following questions:**

a What did you like about this topic?

____

____

____

b What was hard to understand about this topic?

____

____

____

I understand.

I understand a bit.

I need more time to understand this.

3 **Look again at the checklist below. How are you doing now? Circle one face for each statement.**

- I can describe different types of weather.
- I can use symbols and charts to record the weather.

4 **Ask an adult at home to read and sign this.**

I have checked learning on this topic.

We have shared some understanding at home.

Signed: ______________________

Date: ______________

Teacher comment: ______________________________

____

Date: ______________